CITY CYCLING
CHICAGO

Text by Greg Borzo
Illustrations by Michael Valenti

Rapha.

Thames & Hudson

Original concept created by
Andrew Edwards and Max Leonard

This book is dedicated to the Active Transportation Alliance, which for decades has been making Chicago more of a cycling city. Bike advocacy. Bike safety. Bike fun. Active Trans does it all with energy and style. Randy Neufeld got the organization off to a strong start. Today, Executive Director Ron Burke is doing a great job continuing that tradition.

First published in the United Kingdom in 2018 by
Thames & Hudson Ltd, 181A High Holborn, London WC1V 7QX

City Cycling Chicago © 2018 Thames & Hudson Ltd, London

Designed by Michael Lenz, Draught Associates

Illustrations by Michael Valenti

British Library Cataloguing-in-Publication Data
A catalogue record for this book is available from the British Library

ISBN 978-0-500-29310-2

Printed and bound in China by Everbest Printing Co. Ltd

CONTENTS

HOW TO USE THIS GUIDE

This Chicago volume of the *City Cycling* series is designed to give you the confidence to explore the city by bike at your own pace. On the front flaps is a locator map of the whole city to help you orient yourself. Here, you will see five neighbourhoods to explore: Wicker Park (p. 10); Lakefront Path South (p. 16); West Side (p. 22); Lincoln Park (p. 28); and Downtown (p. 34).

Each of these neighbourhoods is easily accessible by bike, and is full of cafés, bars, galleries, museums, shops and parks. All are mapped in detail, and our recommendations for places of interest and where to fuel up on coffee and cake, as well as where to find a WiFi connection, are marked. Take a pootle round on your bike and see what suits you.

If you fancy a set itinerary, turn to A Day On The Bike on the front flaps. It takes you on a relaxed 14-km (9-mile) route through some of the parts of Chicago we haven't featured in the neighbourhood sections, and visits some of the more touristy sights. Pick and choose the bits you fancy, go from back to front, and use the route as you wish.

A section on Racing and Training (p. 40) fills you in on some of Chicago's cycling heritage and provides ideas for longer rides if you want to explore the beautiful countryside around the city, while Essential Bike Info (p. 44) discusses road etiquette and the ins and outs of using the cycle-hire scheme and public transportation. Finally, Links and Addresses (p. 48) will give you the practical details you need to know.

CHICAGO: THE CYCLING CITY

There's never been a better time to bike in Chicago: the Second City is the first in the nation for cycling, according to *Bicycling* magazine's 2016 biennial rating. Several years ago, Chicago set out to increase its bicycle infrastructure and encourage people to cycle. Those efforts have been successful and are leading to still more improvements. Here are a few of the initiatives:

- The 30-km (18.5-mile) Lakefront Path, already the best urban ride in the country, is getting two upgrades, to be completed in 2018. One separates bike and pedestrians along the entire path, and the other is a flyover at the river and Navy Pier, which will eliminate a dangerous chokepoint that requires cyclists to cross two congested streets and share a crowded sidewalk with seemingly thousands of pedestrians.
- Divvy (see p. 46), the country's most successful bike-sharing scheme, continues to expand. With over 5,800 bikes and 580 docking stations, the system has logged more than 11 million rides.
- Chicago has over 400 km (250 miles) – and counting – of on-street bike lanes, almost half of which are protected from automotive traffic by a buffer or barrier. Plus, it has over 80 km (50 miles) of off-street paths, including the 606 (see p. 22) and Lakefront Path (see p. 17).
- A strong bike-to-work movement has led many employers to provide shower facilities and secure bicycle parking to commuters.
- Chicago cyclists benefit from several new laws that make the streets safer. One requires cars to pass bikes with at least 1 m (3 ft) of clearance. Another holds drivers responsible for 'dooring' cyclists. Scores of police patrol the city on bikes, which reinforces the notion that bikes belong.

In addition, a long line of mayors have supported cycling. In 1897, Carter Harrison, Jr ran with the campaign slogan 'not a champion cyclist, but the cyclists' champion' (he won). Both mayor Daleys encouraged cycling, but their successor Rahm Emanuel has been the best friend Chicago cyclists ever had, introducing several schemes and improvements.

Chicago is flat, making it easy to pedal around. It boasts many large parks, all of which (except for Millennium Park) allow cycling on their sidewalks. It supports a strong cycling culture, with umpteen clubs, events, bike-friendly bars and restaurants, film festivals, a bike art fair, Slow Roll rides and a huge Critical Mass following. Chicago is also a leader in bike advocacy, thanks to the Mayor's Bicycle Advisory Council and the Active Transportation Alliance, which has been fighting for the rights of cyclists for over a quarter of a century.

Join this bike-friendly community, if only for a day. You'll enjoy cycling around town and discovering a vibrant, diverse and safe city, one that in many ways is best visited from the saddle of a two-wheeler. This allows you to see things up close, hear the street music, smell the food of Chicago's ethnic neighbourhoods, interact with people and dismount along the way to check out a museum, shop, restaurant, bar or park.

In short, bike the Chicago way: early and often!

NEIGHBOURHOODS

WICKER PARK

HIPSTER HIGHWAY, CHIC BOUTIQUES, COOL CAFÉS

Most of this ride will be spent on Milwaukee Ave, one of the most biked streets in the country, so let's start on the 'Hipster Highway' at the **Iguana Cafe ❶**. It opened in 1998 in Sparta, Greece, but two years later relocated to Chicago, bringing with it a taste of Europe. If the coffee doesn't wake you up, the colours and bright decor will. Load up on crêpes or bagels, waffles or wraps, as you please, then hop on your two-wheeled steed and let your nose guide you to **Blommer Chocolate ❷**, part of North America's largest chocolate supplier. Its retail outlet (open from 9am, Monday–Saturday) sells a variety of chocolate treats that have fuelled many a trek.

While you're on Kinzie Ave, bike its protected lane east to Wells St and back. Opened in 2011, this was Mayor Rahm Emanuel's first bicycle-infrastructure project. Although criticized early on by motorists, it set an ambitious bike-friendly tone for Emanuel's administration, and today the future of the well-used lane seems secure. Head northwest on Milwaukee, where you'll benefit from more protected lanes and cycling infrastructure. And check out Chicago's first public **bike fix-it station ❸**, located next to the Paramount Room. It sports an air pump, bike stand and several tools (tethered to the stand).

Next up is the **Woman Made Gallery** ❹, designed to cultivate female artists by providing exhibition space, professional development and programmes. It's always worth a stop, although you might have to swing back owing to its limited hours. The same is true of the **Polish Museum of America** ❺, the country's largest museum dedicated to a single ethnic group. It harkens back to the days when more Poles lived in Chicago than in Warsaw, when this area was known as Polish Downtown. Ironically, the fountain in the next big intersection (called **Polonia Triangle** ❻) is named after Nelson Algren, who angered local Poles by writing about life in this neighbourhood with gritty, some say exaggerated, realism.

If you're ready for a break, head to **Lovely Kitchen & Cafe** ❼. Lovely, indeed: this refuge exudes calm, enhanced by specialty coffees, teas and homemade treats. As you cycle farther up Milwaukee Ave, you'll find more and more shops, everything from **Value Pawn** ❽, offering a large assortment of goods (and loans), to **Marco Fleseri** ❾, which offers the sort of one-of-a-kind jewelry you'll need a loan to purchase.

Other shops that stand out on this eclectic thoroughfare are **Kokorokoko** ❿, a smart boutique filled with vintage wear from the 1980s and '90s; **Halloween Hallway Costume Shop** ⓫, in case you want to continue your ride incognito; and **Rapha Chicago** ⓬, for continuing

your ride in style. Headquartered in London with a US base in Portland, Oregon, Rapha opened this Chicago outpost in 2016. It doubles as a clubhouse, hosts rides and screens major road races, as well as offering a well-stocked café – plenty of reasons to stop by.

Be sure to head to **Wicker Park** ⓭ itself, a bit off the main drag. In 1868, Charles and Joel Wicker set aside four acres of underdeveloped land for a park to enhance local real-estate values. It worked, and their legacy is this beautiful park at the centre of one of Chicago's most vibrant residential communities. Ground Zero for the Wicker Park neighbourhood, as well as Chicago's urban cycling scene, is the intersection of North Ave and Milwaukee. A stone's throw from here you'll find several bars, cafés and stores. **Myopic** ⓮, one of the best used bookstores anywhere, boasts a huge selection of well-organized books and doesn't have the dusty, musty feel of many other used bookstores. If you're more into 'zines, graphic novels and alternative publications, visit **Quimby's** ⓯, a funky shop where you never know what you'll find, but whatever you do is sure to be provocative or amusing.

There are plenty of high-end fashionable shops nearby, along the lines of **Steve Madden** ⓰, **Club Monaco** ⓱ and **Oak + Fort** ⓲. But if you'd rather spin than shop, truck a couple of blocks north and jump on the 606 (see p. 22), a 4.3-km (2.7-mile) elevated bike path described in the West Side ride. This would add some serious pedalling to an otherwise slow roll.

Now that the Paramount Room (near our starting point) is open, make your way to this bicycle-friendly restaurant/bar to dine on mussels or oysters, pork belly or steak tartare, or any of its other delicacies. Afterwards, sip cocktails and catch a performance at **Davenport's Piano Bar and Cabaret ⑲**, an intimate lounge with stage shows, cabaret singers, comedians, open mic and karaoke. The piano's up front and the cabaret's at the back of this swanky lair, a throwback to the 1950s, which is also surprisingly up to date.

REFUELLING

FOOD
Big Star ⑳, a beer-and-bourbon honky-tonk in a 1940s gas station
Piece Brewery & Pizzeria ㉑ – beer and pizza, what more do you need?

DRINK
Don't miss **Revolution Brewing ㉒**, where the hardcore cyclists hang out
Buzz: Killer Espresso ㉓ brews great coffee and chai latte

WIFI
Volumes Bookcafe ㉔ offers plenty of tables to park yourself with coffee and books

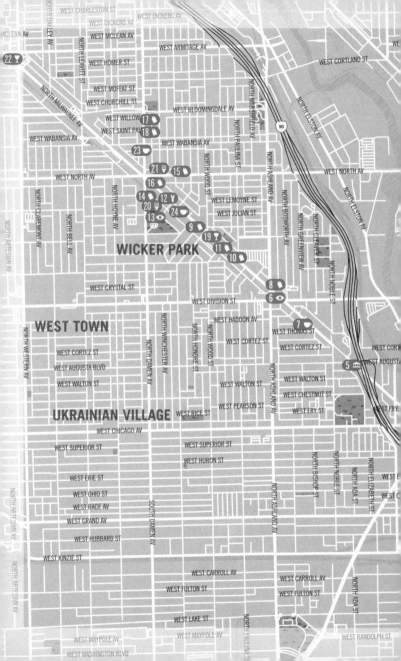

LAKEFRONT PATH SOUTH

MUSEUMS, HYDE PARK, UNIVERSITY OF CHICAGO

Chicagoans are known for boasting, but it's no exaggeration to say that the Lakefront Path is the most beautiful urban ride in the country – if you like water, greenery, museums, restaurants, beaches, boats and people-watching, that is. This path has it all. Many other cities have lost their waterfronts to industrial and transportation facilities, but Chicago's visionary forefathers tenaciously defended virtually all of the lakefront for parks and people. And major infrastructure improvements keep making the Lakefront Path safer and easier to navigate.

Let's begin our day with breakfast at **Spoke & Bird** ❶, an excellent bike-oriented restaurant serving basic American fare, where roadies gather on the large patio. Before saddling up, visit the adjacent Women's Park and Gardens, a peaceful sanctuary that's home to the **Henry B. Clarke House** ❷, built in 1836 and Chicago's oldest residence. Now a museum, the house sits back from Prairie Ave, Chicago's original Gold Coast, back when the likes of businessmen and entrepreneurs Potter Palmer and Marshall Field lived here. Some of the historic mansions, including the massive Glessner House, still display that Gilded Age opulence.

Ride towards the lake on 18th St, past the site of the Battle of Fort Dearborn, and follow the curved **bike/pedestrian bridge** ❸ over the railroad tracks. Bike northeast past Soldier Field, with its odd, flying saucer-like addition, and continue until you hit the Lakefront Path. Visit at least one of the outstanding attractions of the splendid Museum Campus, created in 1998. You've got plenty to choose from: the **Field Museum of Natural History** ❹, **Shedd Aquarium** ❺ or **Adler Planetarium** ❻. All three were part of the Century of Progress in 1933–4, Chicago's second World's Fair, which celebrated the city's 100th birthday and helped lift the nation out of the Great Depression.

Next, cruise past McCormick Place, an enormous, monolithic convention centre. Note all the boats along the way: Chicago, with 10 harbours, has more privately registered boats than any other US city. But there's plenty of nature along the way, too. Watch out for prairie-restoration projects named for Daniel Burnham, Chicago's favourite architect, who was famous for saying, 'Make no little plans; they have no magic to stir men's blood.' Burnham followed his own advice, supervising the construction of the World's Columbian Exposition of 1893 (described in the 2003 book *Devil in the White City*) and co-authoring the 1909 Plan of Chicago. Much of what you see during these rides originated in one of these schemes.

For lunch, exit the path at 53rd St and find your way to **Bonjour Cafe Bakery 7**, which serves soups, croissants and French pastries that taste even better than they look. Across the small plaza sits **DJ's Bike Doctor 8**, a shop known for good, honest service for almost 40 years.

Next, bike to the **Museum of Science and Industry 9**, renowned for its planes, trains and automobiles, as well as a coal mine, U-boat, old-time Main St and exhibit of hatching chicks. This interactive museum makes learning fun, and is one of the few buildings left over from the World's Columbian Exposition, where it served as the Palace of Fine Arts. The fair stretched from 56th to 67th streets, covering much of Jackson Park. If you're adventurous, track down **Wooded Island 10**, an asylum during the fair and home of a serene Japanese Temple that contrasted starkly with the hubbub and enormity of the fair's other exhibits. The island, best approached from the north, has just been beautifully restored.

Swing by **5046 S Greenwood Ave ⑪**, Barack Obama's Chicago home, although you may not be allowed to get close, then amble through the University of Chicago, where he taught constitutional law. This distinguished campus is known for its Gothic buildings, including **Rockefeller Chapel ⑫**. It's also dotted with an increasing number of modern structures, such as the domed **Mansueto Library ⑬**. North of the library, find *Nuclear Energy,* a bronze sculpture on the site of the world's first nuclear reaction. Then tour Frank Lloyd Wright's **Robie House ⑭**, a stunning example of Prairie School architecture.

Just off campus but virtually part of the university is **57th Street Books ⑮**, a stellar independent bookstore. From there, pick up the mile-long **Midway Plaisance ⑯**, which connects Jackson and Washington parks. It was the playground of the World's Columbian Exposition, full of carnival rides and exotic entertainment, including the hoochie-coochie girls. The first ever Ferris Wheel turned on the spot where you now see a **skating rink ⑰**.

Bike west to Lorado Taft's dark **Fountain of Time ⑱**, a sculpture that shows humanity marching past an ominous, unforgiving Father Time. Hyde Park is not known for fine dining, but the laid-back **Medici on 57th ⑲** is solid. Open since 1962, it's the go-to place for locals, as well as for students and teachers (plus, it's BYOB). The park isn't known for its nightlife, either, but the **Court Theatre ⑳** is top-notch. Affiliated with the university, this professional theatre is dedicated to innovation, intellectual engagement and community service.

REFUELLING

FOOD
La Petite Folie ㉑ serves classic French dishes in a serene atmosphere
Valois ㉒ is a classic cafeteria with an old-time buzz

DRINK
The Promontory ㉓ offers exotic cocktails and musical performances
Cove Lounge ㉔ is a relaxed saloon with foosball, darts and cheap drinks

WIFI
Overflow Coffee Bar ㉕ is a community centre out to change the world – plus it has free WiFi

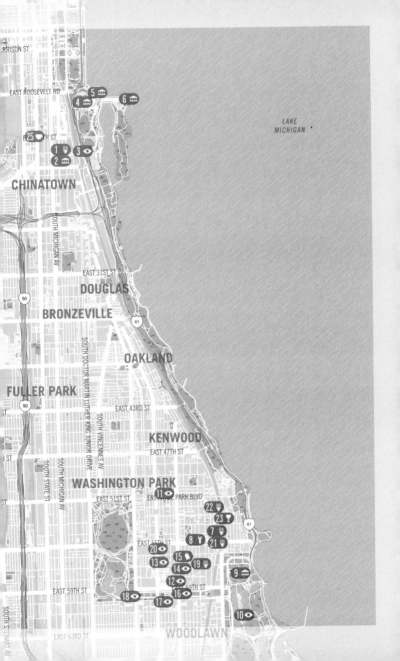

WEST SIDE

BOULEVARDS, LOGAN SQUARE, ELEVATED 606 PATH

Start the day off right with breakfast at **Milk & Honey ❶**, which has both homemade pastries and six different flavours of granola on offer. You'll need to be fortified for our next stop: **Shit Fountain ❷**. Just what it says on the tin, this 'pile of crap' was created by Jerzy Kenar, an artist better known for liturgical furnishings than 'poop'-ular art. What made him build this, you ask? Well, after many of his neighbours failed to pick up after their dogs, Kenar decided to erect a not-so-subtle reminder in front of his home/studio.

Proceed west on Augusta Blvd, a relatively quiet street with a clearly marked bike lane. Notice all the two-flats, bungalows and modest storefronts: this is quintessential Chicago. After about 2.5 km (1.5 miles) you'll hit **Humboldt Park ❸**. Tool around this grand urban retreat and stop for a beverage at the pleasant **Boathouse Cafe ❹**. Boats no longer adorn the lagoon, but the view of the water is great from the terrace. The park is also home to the **Puerto Rican Arts Alliance ❺**, a museum and community centre dedicated to preserving Puerto Rican culture.

After you get your fill of the park, bike two blocks north on Humboldt Blvd to catch the **606 ❻**, a new elevated linear park that runs east–west, parallel to Bloomingdale Ave, and so named because every Chicagoan's zip code begins with those numbers. To access it, pass underneath the park and turn east up the entrance ramp. This phenomenal urban space has a 4.3-km (2.7-mile) path for walkers and cyclists, and is a true unifier, welcoming all and linking diverse neighbourhoods. Head east on the 606, because it's time for lunch and you can't beat **Hot Chocolate ❼**, just a few doors south on Damen Ave. You won't regret whatever you order at this casual yet stylish restaurant, but be sure to get a cup of its namesake cocoa and one of the scrumptious desserts.

Back on the 606, boogie east to the end and then all the way back to the western end (both off-map). That way you'll be able to say you rode the entire distance of this, the country's longest and most welcoming elevated rails-to-trail path. Yes, it's cooler than New York's ballyhooed High Line, which doesn't even allow bicycles! The western portion of the 606 shows off the city's industrial heritage, while the eastern side displays the tastes of

the hip residents moving into the area. Jump off the 606 anywhere along the way to explore one of the several adjacent street-level parks, most of which have playgrounds and picnic areas. At Kimball Ave, there's **Archery Bow Range** ❽, the local source for urban archery. It offers classes, events and a shooting range for training, but check the hours: this quirky place is not always open.

After finishing your loop on the 606, alight back on Humboldt Blvd. This verdant road is part of a 45-km (28-mile) green belt that virtually encircles the city's core and connects seven large parks. After half a mile, follow the boulevard west along the elegant **Palmer Square** ❾, then turn north on Kedzie Blvd. Soon you'll hit **Logan Square** ❿, a wonderfully diverse and energetic neighbourhood and a magnet for millennials. Its cool vibe has attracted umpteen smart shops, including **City Lit Books** ⓫, a classy yet cosy bookstore dedicated to helping you find that 'special book that changes your understanding of the world around you'. The **Logan Square Farmers Market** ⓬, one of the city's most dynamic, is held on Sunday mornings, almost year round. (From November to March, it heads indoors at 2755 N Milwaukee.) If your tyres are low or your bike needs a quick repair, drop in on **Boulevard Bikes** ⓭ for first-rate service and sales.

Logan Square Park, at the heart of the neighbourhood, features two interesting sights. Easy to find is the **Illinois Centennial Monument** ⓮, built in 1918 to celebrate the 100th anniversary of Illinois' statehood. This 9 m (30 ft)-tall Doric column, topped with an eagle, was designed by Henry Bacon, who also designed the Lincoln Memorial in Washington, DC. A bit harder to find is the **Comfort Station** ⓯, a cute Tudor-style cabin built in 1927 for transit riders to rest, use the washroom and seek shelter from the weather. Abandoned in the 1940s, the building is lucky to have escaped demolition. In 2005 it was restored and now hosts art exhibits, musical performances and outdoor film screenings.

Cap off your day with dinner at **Lula Cafe** ⓰, a funky restaurant with an inventive, market-driven menu. Many nightspots grace the area, including **Billy Sunday** ⓱, which serves upscale cocktails and gastropub fare. There's something enticing about enjoying a strong drink in a bar named after the evangelical preacher who 'couldn't shut down that Toddlin' Town', at least according to the lyrics of the 1922 song *Chicago*, most famously sung by Frank Sinatra.

REFUELLING

FOOD	DRINK
Reno Chicago ⓲ for wood-fired bagels and pizza	**Big Shoulders Coffee** ⓴ for a great cuppa Joe
Dunlays on the Square ⓳, a happening bar and grill, with patio seating	**Webster's Wine Bar** ㉑, a romantic hideout with 600 varieties of vino fino

WIFI
The funky, spacious **New Wave Coffee** ㉒ is the place to go for local coffee (Metropolis) and a large selection of tea

LINCOLN PARK

STYLISH NEIGHBOURHOOD, LAKEFRONT PARK, ZOO

With so many awesome eateries in this part of town, why not try two options for breakfast? **Nookies ❶**, a local fave since 1973, opens at 6:3Øam and does a great job with traditional American dishes. The **Original Pancake House ❷** is a chain but does everything right, from the decor to the service, crêpes to waffles, and – oh yes – pancakes.

Work off those calories by biking north on Stockton Dr to the **Lincoln Park Conservatory ❸**, a Victorian greenhouse with individual rooms for ferns, orchids, show plants and tropical plants. Around the corner on Fullerton Ave is the entrance to a hidden gem, the **Alfred Caldwell Lily Pool ❹**, a lush, tranquil garden designed to resemble the banks of a river meandering through a bucolic Midwestern setting.

Take the rest of the morning to explore **Lincoln Park Zoo ❺**, one of the few major zoos in the country with free admission. If you've got kids in tow, or are just a kid at heart, don't miss the Pritzker Family Children's Zoo and Farm-in-the-Zoo. Follow this up with lunch and a beer at **Cafe Brauer ❻**, a handsome Prairie School-style building from 1908 next to the North Pond. Or, for a better meal but less of a view, skip around the corner to **R.J. Grunts ❼**, the first restaurant opened by the Lettuce Entertain You group, and known for its fun atmosphere and massive salad bar, with over 50 items on offer.

Afterwards, stroll the Nature Boardwalk through a restored prairie ecosystem, a refuge for birds and butterflies, fish and frogs. Amble through Lincoln Park until you come across the exquisite **Standing Lincoln ❽**, a statue of that giant among men for whom the park is named. Created by Augustus Saint-Gaudens, one of America's greatest sculptors, it shows the 16th president in a contemplative pose, made especially realistic by the use of a life mask of his face and casts of his hands.

Discover more about Lincoln at the Chicago History Museum (see A Day On The Bike), just a few turns of your pedals westward. This highly regarded institution traces the city's development from western outpost in the 1830s to trendsetting metropolis. Learn about Chicago as the Crossroads of America, discover its writers and take the Fifth Star Challenge. The four stars on the Chicago flag represent the Great Chicago Fire, the World's Columbian Exposition, the Century of Progress and the Battle of Fort Dearborn, each of which is covered at the museum. As you ride this book's routes, keep your eyes open for locations, buildings and references to these seminal events – and think about what other event might warrant a fifth star on the city flag.

Jaunt west to Wells St to experience Old Town. In the 1960s, this area was a hippie hangout and folk-music haven. Today, it's an eclectic neighbourhood that has gone upscale, owing to the increasingly affluent residents living here in restored Victorian houses, stone mansions and deluxe condos. As you cycle south on the bustling bike lane, many shops beckon you to part with your time and your cash. For excellent coffee and a fine choice of tea, stop at **Le Pain Quotidien ❾**, or, if you have a sweet tooth, head to the **Fudge Pot ❿**, which has been making Chicago sweeter since 1963 with handmade confectionery creations. A couple doors further down is the **Spice House ⓫**, which – you guessed it – has been making Chicago spicier since 1957.

For gifts, a good option is **Judy Maxwell Home ⑫**, a nostalgic shop arranged like a general store that sells practical, amusing, even 'slightly inappropriate', items. **Village Cycle Center ⑬**, a one-stop shop for all your biking needs, boasts Chicago's largest selection of bikes and types of bikes, while down the road, **J.C. Lind Bike Co. ⑭** specializes in sturdy yet elegant Dutch bikes. (Yes, the Dutch know a thing or two about two-wheeling!)

As it's getting close to dinner time, indulge yourself with a glass of wine at the **Glunz Tavern ⑮**. Next door is the House of Glunz, Chicago's oldest family-owned wine shop, founded in 1888. If you prefer to BYOB, choose a bottle from the shop's fine selection and swing back to **Cafe Sushi ⑯**, one of the city's top Japanese restaurants. Or if you'd rather consult a wine list, head to **Topo Gigio ⑰**, which features a superb modern Tuscan cuisine and charming outdoor seating.

Afterwards, take in a laugh riot at the legendary **Second City ⑱**, the improvisational comedy club that launched the careers of John Belushi, Gilda Radner, Bill Murray, and other greats. For something more raucous, hit **Zanies Comedy Club ⑲**, an intimate venue that has featured some of the country's best standup comedians, including Jay Leno and Jerry Seinfeld. After the show, catch a nightcap at **Fireplace Inn ⑳**, also known for its barbeque. Or try your luck at the typically packed **Old Town Pour House ㉑**, an upscale bar with a lively buzz. This trendy 'homage to beer' offers mezzanine seating, lots of big-screen TVs and 90 beers on tap.

REFUELLING

FOOD	DRINK
3rd Coast Cafe & Wine Bar ㉒ is open 7am to midnight every day	**Old Town Ale House ㉔** was film critic Roger Ebert's favourite bar
Mon Ami Gabi ㉓ for an authentic French brasserie experience	**Bourgeois Pig Cafe ㉕** features a 'drip du jour' and a great selection of teas

WIFI

Cocoa + Co. Cafe and Coffee Shop ㉖ caters to life's most pressing needs – for coffee and chocolate

DOWNTOWN

THE LOOP, THE L, PRINTERS ROW, SHOPPING

Start off with breakfast at the wildly popular **Wildberry Pancakes &
Cafe ❶**. Good thing it opens at 6:30am, because there's so much to
discover downtown. If your tastes run to continental, head instead to
Toni Patisserie & Cafe ❷, which serves French-style sweets and savouries.
After fuelling up, visit the exquisite **Chicago Cultural Center ❸**, built in
1897 as the main public library. Believe it or not, this Renaissance palace
came close to being demolished.

Head west on Randolph St underneath Chicago's biggest mover
and shaker, the 'L'. This 19th-century elevated transit system covers the
city and defines downtown as the 'Loop'. It's an antique, alright, but a
working one that carries more riders every year. Turn north on State St
towards the newly developed **Chicago Riverwalk ❹**, a lively celebration
of water, architecture and the good life. Take the stairs or look for the

entrance ramp at LaSalle St. Biking is permitted, but the path is often crowded with pedestrians. For years, the river was ignored and viewed as little more than a water alley. Today, its banks are alive with restaurants, bars and festivals. Take State St back south to see the iconic marquee of the **Chicago Theatre ❺**, one of many grand venues in the vibrant Theater District. Jockey over to Dearborn St and cycle south along the award-winning lane that's part of Chicago's vast and growing network of bikeways. Watch out for pedestrians, though: they won't be expecting bikes coming south on this one-way, northbound street, so use your bell freely.

Plan to stop all along Dearborn St for the astonishing assortment of outdoor art and architecture. First, on your right, is the International-style **Richard J. Daley Center ❻**. Out front is the enigmatic 'Chicago Picasso', an untitled gift from the artist: go ahead, slide down the front! And soak your feet in the fountain on the other side of the plaza. Every year, this plaza hosts the energetic Bike to Work Rally, when thousands of cyclists cap off a competition that encourages people to commute by bike. By now you've earned coffee at **Cochon Volant** **❼**, an attractive French brasserie. For something stronger, how about lunch and suds at the landmark **Berghoff** **❽**? Just don't expect your beer to cost a nickel, like it did when this old-world German restaurant/brewery opened in 1898.

Back on your mechanical horse, ride past **Chase Tower** **❾** with its wide base, built to accommodate the scores of tellers back when branch banking was illegal in Chicago and before ATMs had been invented. Take a minute to cool off in the fountain in the sunken plaza and admire Marc Chagall's mosaic, **Four Seasons** **❿**. Next up is the striking **Flamingo** **⓫** by Alexander Calder, an artist better known for his mobiles. The curvy structure contrasts with the squared-off plaza and ominous black buildings of the surrounding Federal Center, designed by Mies Van der Rohe. Another block south is the **MCC Chicago** **⓬**, a tall, triangular building with narrow windows. Just don't ask to tour it, though: it's a federal prison!

Cross Congress Parkway, and you're in Printer's Row, a former printing and publishing district. The 'untouchable' Eliot Ness had his office in the **Transportation Building** **⓭**, at the north end of Printer's Row Park. Formerly a parking lot surrounded by rundown buildings, this tiny space was transformed by community members into a well-designed public park. **Dearborn Station** **⓮**, the last of several 19th-century downtown rail terminals, stands tall at the end of Dearborn St. Behind it, where a gaggle of tracks once converged, is a secluded housing development. Cycle through it to experience a tranquil, residential side to big-city life.

Students are also embracing Loop living. In fact, downtown Chicago is the nation's largest college town, with more than 60,000 students living – and contributing to the dynamic cycling culture – within a one-mile radius of State St and Congress Pkwy. Visit the **State Street Gallery** ⓯ at Robert Morris University, which is free and open to the public, and walk through the lobby of Louis Sullivan's **Auditorium Building** ⓰, built in 1893 and now occupied by Roosevelt University. You'll see more evidence of students as you cycle along Wabash Ave, a burgeoning arts corridor with sculptures and murals.

To put a few more points on your Fitbit, cruise south on Wabash Ave until you hit Interstate 55. There's plenty to see along the way, the traffic's light and the bike lane is wide. Dine at the fun, deli-style **Eleven City Diner** ⓱, a high-quality, old-fashioned eatery. Or try **Lou Malnati's** ⓲ for the best deep-dish pizza in a town known for pizza. Chicago is also known for the blues, and a hotspot for that is **Buddy Guy's Legends** ⓳, where Buddy himself occasionally sings. If you prefer jazz, head to the intimate Jazz Showcase, which has been showcasing great performers since 1947. Top off the evening at **Cindy's** ⓴, a cool new bar overlooking Millennium Park from the 22nd floor of the storied Chicago Athletic Club. There are also bars and a game room on the lower floors of this happening place, recently refurbished by local billionaire Cindy Pritzker.

REFUELLING

FOOD

Sofi Restaurant ㉑ is an upscale trattoria in the heart of prestigious Printer's Row
The Art Deco **Ceres Cafe** ㉒ offers tasty food in the Board of Trade building

DRINK

Tea café **Argo Tea** ㉓ also offers coffee and snacks
Tutto Italiano ㉔ is a fine restaurant/bar inside a quaint old railcar

WIFI

Harold Washington Library ㉕ has plenty of seats and the best WiFi in town – no food allowed, but you can bring in a covered drink

ST

RIO ST 15 Ⓦ 16 ⊟ 17 ◉ 18 ◗

ST OHIO ST

EAST GRAND AV

13 ◉   12 ⊟   11 Ⓦ   14 ◉

10 ◉

OIS ST

RVICE DRIVE

WATERSIDE DRIVE

ST SIDE

ON PLACE

RANDOLPH ST   8 ◉

LAKE
MICHIGAN

MCFETRIDGE DRIVE

RACING & TRAINING

Chicago is a prime location for many kinds of bicycle racing, from track to road races and from alleycats to cyclocross to criteriums. Most of these races have multiple levels. The **Intelligentsia Cup** – a multi-day omnium road race powered by Chicago-based SRAM, one of the largest bike-component manufacturers in the country – includes a junior category to encourage young new riders to compete. So don't be intimidated by the Spandex, experienced cyclists or expensive bikes: just ride.

If you're already a Category-1 or professional racer, be assured that you'll find plenty of stiff competition on sanctioned events. The **Illinois Cycling Association**, the local branch of USA Cycling, does a lot to support cyclists and racing programmes throughout the state. Local races and group rides are posted and tracked by **Chicago Bike Racing**, which maintains a directory of local teams. It also hosts a blog that covers news about Chicago road racing.

Many clubs, breweries and bike shops host teams. One of the most successful is **xXx Racing-Athletico**, a Chicago-based amateur racing team, and one of the best known is the **Chicago Cycling Club**, which offers training and recreational rides. Among the most legendary is the **University of Chicago Velo Club**, a Division-2 collegiate racing team that hosts the annual Monsters of the Midway criterium around (and around) the Midway Plaisance. ('Midway' refers to a boulevard near the University of Chicago; 'Monsters of the Midway' was originally the nickname of the university's football team, but has since been adopted by the Chicago Bears.)

The Windy City has a long tradition of bicycle racing, going back to the historic Pullman Bicycle Race, which in the 1890s attracted up to 300 riders. (This classic ride has recently been revived.) During the same era, punishing six-day races were popular at the Chicago Coliseum and outdoor tracks around the city, including one on the South Side that was part of the World's Columbian Exposition in 1893. At another outdoor track in Garfield Park, Marshall 'Major' Taylor, one of the great racers of all time, set several world records. He was the first black athlete to win a world championship and to be a member of an integrated professional sports team in the United States. A trail on the South Side is named in his honour.

Today, Chicagoland racers can still train on outdoor tracks. The suburb of Northbrook proudly sports the **Ed Rudolph Velodrome**, one of the few velodromes left in the country. This quarter-mile track with 18° banked turns opened in 1960 and is run by the local park district, which ensures it is available for anyone to ride daily – on any kind of bike. (The banks are gentle, so give it a try.) Of course, certain times are reserved for training, races and other events. The park maintains an active schedule, and its races attract professional cyclists, as well as sizeable crowds of spectators.

Almost 100 km (60 miles) north of Chicago is the **Washington Park Velodrome**, which opened in 1927, making it the oldest operating velodrome in the country. Find this historic treasure – but still active racing site – at Washington Rd and 22nd Ave in Kenosha, Wisconsin.

Chicago is flat, but many suburban areas are blessed with hilly terrain. For some quad-crunching climbs, check out the **Moraine Hills State Park** in Holiday Hills, about 80 km (50 miles) from the Loop. The **Waterfall Glen Forest Trail**, which circles the Argonne National Laboratory in

Lemont, 39 km (24 miles) from the Loop, also serves up a couple of hills. For additional climbing, try a multilevel parking garage, any of which come with ramps that are sure to elevate your heart rate – although the scenery won't be as uplifting as that along the Lakefront Path. And for a rugged mountain bike experience, cruise over to the **Palos Forest Preserve Trail** in Willow Springs, 35 km (22 miles) from the Loop. This amazing 15,000-acre preserve provides more than 32 km (20 miles) of trails, including Chicagoland's roughest, toughest dirt trails.

Then there's **Big Marsh Park,** a heavenly bike training and recreational area that opened on the South Side, 24 km (15 miles) from the Loop, in 2016. There you'll find multipurpose trails, single tracks, pump tracks (large and small), a tot track, wooden ramps, sand pits and a Cyclocross course, including Belgian stairs. This treasure was carved out of a former industrial wasteland. The restoration work continues, and more bicycle amenities are being added. **The Garden,** a modest BMX playground on the North Side, is also worth visiting. This free open course features three jump lines and a pump track with multiple routes. The entire assembly was built and continues to be maintained by volunteers. Find it in the Richard Clark Playlot Park, just north of Belmont Ave along the North Branch of the Chicago River.

Dozens of parks and forest preserves in and around the city offer serious training and stunning recreational riding. Many of these sites are surprisingly bucolic, including the **Des Plaines River Trail** through Lake County, about 48 km (30 miles) from the Loop, which features well-maintained underpasses and crushed limestone surfaces. West of the city, the fabulous rails-to-trails **Illinois Prairie Path**, centred in Wheaton, 47 km (29 miles) from the Loop, offers mile upon mile of straightaways on crushed limestone. For a long, straight paved path with relatively few road crossings, head to the **Old Plank Road Trail** from Park Forest, 16 km (10 miles) from the Loop, to Joliet.

But whatever you do, don't train on the Lakefront Path when it's busy, because there are just too many pedestrians, joggers, in-line skaters, Segway riders, dogs, beachcombers, skateboarders, vendors, and more. Long and far may you bike!

ESSENTIAL BIKE INFO

Cycling in Chicago is safe and straightforward. The city is flat,
streets are wide and sightlines are clear. In the past few years,
bicycling has become more popular than ever, so you'll have plenty
of two-wheeled companions.

ETIQUETTE

The layout of Chicago's streets does not encourage aggressive driving. Drivers
tend to be courteous, but some of them are a bit touchy about the fact that
they have to share the road. You'll get along fine with them as long as you
follow the rules. Stop at red lights and stop signs, and don't cycle against
traffic. Establish eye contact when you need to make a move. And why not
smile and wave at drivers? Think of yourself as an ambassador for all the
cyclists who will follow in your tyre tracks.

Be especially courteous to pedestrians, as they are more vulnerable than
cyclists. If you're over 11 years old, you're not allowed to bike on the sidewalk,
even when that looks like your safest option.

TRAFFIC SAFETY

The most important thing for cyclists (and drivers) to remember is to avoid
distractions. This means do not use your mobile phone while biking, or wear
headphones or ear buds that compromise your ability to connect with your
surroundings.

As you cycle, remember: you are traffic. Bike in a predictable manner
and be aware of the vehicles around you. Ride at least 1 m (3 ft away) from
parked cars, so you won't get 'doored', even if you have to take the lane. Bike
single file, and on the right. It's better to follow buses and trucks than to
try passing them, because they often don't see cyclists when they turn right
or swing over to the curb. Streets have many potholes, so focus on the road
ahead, rather than the shops and sights along the way. Helmets are highly
recommended, and lights (white at the front and a red reflector, at the very
least, at the back) are required after sunset.

One thing that is tricky to negotiate when cycling in Chicago is the six-corner intersection, where a big angle street hits the junction of two major thoroughfares. Be careful when navigating these crossroads. For a novice, it would be safest to walk your bike around the edge, crossing one street at a time, rather than trying to sail through the middle of the intersection.

SECURITY

As in any big American city, bike theft is an issue in Chicago. Always lock your bike to something secure – not a chain-link fence, or a 'sucker pole' that has been disconnected from its base so thieves can lift the pole to release your locked bike. Thieves look for the easiest bikes to steal, so make it difficult to steal yours by using two locks (preferably of different types) and tying your wheels to the frame. Never lock your bike to a decorative fence in a park or around a building or tree. The city and property owners are allowed to remove and impound such bikes.

There are certain parts of town where you should not bike, especially alone or after dark. The routes in this book avoid such areas.

FINDING YOUR WAY

Chicago is easy to navigate because it's laid out like a piece of graph paper, oriented to the cardinal directions. The corner of State and Madison is the centre from which all streets radiate, eight blocks to a mile (or 16 short, half-blocks). All streets are associated with a number that tells you how far they are from Ground Zero. As long as you keep that and the location of the lake (to the east) in mind, you'll always know where you are.

For example, the intersection of Fullerton Ave (2400 N) and Halsted St (800 W) is 5 km (3 miles) north and 2 km (1 mile) west of State and Madison. The occasional angle streets keep things interesting, but it's easy to mentally overlay them on the grid.

BIKE SHARING AND RENTAL

Chicago runs the country's biggest and best bike-sharing programme. **Divvy** has 5,800 bikes and 580 docking stations – and counting. Use your credit card at any docking station to buy a 24-hour pass, which will allow you to take an unlimited number of 30-minute rides. The three-speed bikes are heavy and slow (clunky), which prevents users from hot-rodding around town. That also makes them sturdier and able to withstand potholes, rain and snow. And yes, the system is available year round, 24/7.

You can also rent a set of wheels, particularly in touristic areas. **Bike and Roll** and **Bobby's Bike Hike** charge about £28 ($35) a day for a basic bike, more for a fancier steed. A surrey cycle, which seats two to six riders, starts at £24 ($30) an hour or £96 ($120) a day.

PUBLIC TRANSIT

Chicago is the envy of the country owing to its 'L', a 160 km (100 mile)-plus rail-transit system. It allows bikes onboard for free, two bikes per car, except for 7–9am and 4–6pm on weekdays. A few times a year, such as July 4, bikes are prohibited owing to the huge number of riders. It's easy to take your bike on the 'L', thanks to accessible turnstiles and lifts in many stations, but bikes are not allowed on escalators.

Bikes also ride for free on the front of city buses, with easy-to-use fold-down racks. It's not permitted to lock your bike to the rack, but lock your wheel to your frame to make it impossible for someone to ride off on your mount. So, if you get a flat or stray too far afield, just give your bike a ride on public transit.

If you fly to Chicago with a bike, don't plan on cycling into town. The roads on the way in are too busy and confusing. A better option would be to take your bike on the 'L', which serves both **O'Hare** and **Midway** airports. **Amtrak**, which also allows bikes on trains (check the rules and restrictions), operates out of downtown's **Union Station**.

LINKS & ADDRESSES

3RD COAST CAFE & WINE BAR
1260 N Dearborn St,
Chicago, IL 60610
3rdcoastcafe.com

57TH STREET BOOKS
1301 E 57th St,
Chicago, IL 60637
57th.semcoop.com

606
the606.org

ADLER PLANETARIUM
Museum Campus,
1300 S Lake Shore Dr,
Chicago, IL 60605
adlerplanetarium.org

ALFRED CALDWELL LILY POOL
125 W Fullerton Pkwy,
Chicago, IL 60614
lincolnparkconservancy.org/projects/
alfred-caldwell-lily-pool/

ARCHERY BOW RANGE
1757 N Kimball Ave,
Chicago, IL 60647
archerybowrangechicago.com

ARGO TEA
1 S Franklin St,
Chicago, IL 60606
argotea.com

ART INSTITUTE OF CHICAGO
111 S Michigan Ave,
Chicago, IL 60603
artic.edu

ATWOOD
The Alise Chicago,
1 W Washington St,
Chicago, IL 60602
atwoodrestaurant.com

AUDITORIUM BUILDING
50 E Congress Pkwy,
Chicago, IL 60605
auditoriumtheatre.org

BERGHOFF
17 W Adams St,
Chicago, IL 60603
theberghoff.com

BIG SHOULDERS COFFEE
1105 W Chicago Ave,
Chicago, IL 60642
bigshoulderscoffee.com

BIG STAR
1531 N Damen Ave,
Chicago, IL 60622
bigstarchicago.com

BILLY SUNDAY
3143 W Logan Blvd,
Chicago, IL 60647
billy-sunday.com

BLOMMER CHOCOLATE
600 Kinzie St,
Chicago, IL 60654
blommer.com

BOATHOUSE CAFE
Humboldt Park Boathouse,
1301 N Sacramento Ave,
Chicago, IL 60622

BONJOUR CAFE BAKERY
1550 E 55th St,
Chicago, IL 60615
facebook.com/Bonjour-Cafe-
Bakery-113471275353073

BOURGEOIS PIG CAFE
738 W Fullerton Ave,
Chicago, IL 60614
bpigcafe.com

BUCKINGHAM FOUNTAIN
501 S Columbus Dr,
Chicago, IL 60605
chicagoparkdistrict.com/parks/
clarence-f-buckingham-memorial-
fountain

BUDDY GUY'S LEGENDS
700 S Wabash Ave,
Chicago, IL 60605
buddyguy.com

BUZZ: KILLER ESPRESSO
1644 N Damen Ave,
Chicago, IL 60647
facebook.com/Buzz.killer.espresso

CAFE BRAUER
2021 N Stockton Dr,
Chicago, IL 60614

CAFE IBERICO
737 N LaSalle Dr,
Chicago, IL 60654
cafeiberico.com

CAFE SUSHI
1342 N Wells St,
Chicago, IL 60610
cafesushiwells.com

CENTENNIAL WHEEL
600 E Grand Ave,
Chicago, IL 60611
navypier.com/centennial-wheel

CERES CAFE
141 W Jackson Blvd,
Chicago, IL 60604
cerescafechicago.com

CHASE TOWER
10 S Dearborn St,
Chicago, IL 60603
chase.com

**CHICAGO ARCHITECTURE
FOUNDATION**
224 S Michigan Ave,
Chicago, IL 60604
architecture.org

CHICAGO CHILDREN'S MUSEUM
700 E Grand Ave,
Chicago, IL 60611
chicagochildrensmuseum.org

CHICAGO CULTURAL CENTER
78 E Washington St,
Chicago, IL 60602
cityofchicago.org/city/en/depts/dca/
supp.../chicago_culturalcenter

CHICAGO HISTORY MUSEUM
1601 N Clark St,
Chicago, IL 60614
chicagohistory.org

CHICAGO RIVERWALK
Chicago, IL 60601
chicagoriverwalk.us

CHICAGO THEATRE
175 N State St,
Chicago, IL 60601
thechicagotheatre.com

CINDY'S
12 Michigan Ave,
Chicago, IL 60603
cindysrooftop.com

CITY LIT BOOKS
2523 N Kedzie Blvd,
Chicago, IL 60647
citylitbooks.com

CLOUD GATE
Chicago, IL 60601
cityofchicago.org/city/en/depts/dca/
supp_info/chicago_s_publicart-
cloudgateinmillenniumpark

CLUB MONACO
1731 N Damen Ave,
Chicago, IL 60647
clubmonaco.com

COCHON VOLANT
100 W Monroe St,
Chicago, IL 60603
cochonvolantchicago.com

**COCOA + CO.
CAFE AND COFFEE SHOP**
1651 N Wells St,
Chicago, IL 60614
cocoaandco.com/pages/cocoa-
co-café

COLUMBIA YACHT CLUB
111 N Lake Shore Dr,
Chicago, IL 60601
columbiayachtclub.org

COMFORT STATION
2579 N Milwaukee Ave,
Chicago, IL 60647
comfortstationlogansquare.org

COURT THEATRE
5535 S Ellis Ave,
Chicago, IL 60637
courttheatre.org

COVE LOUNGE
1750 E 55th St,
Chicago, IL 60615
thecovelounge.com

CROWN FOUNTAIN
Millennium Park,
201 E Randolph St,
Chicago, IL 60602
cityofchicago.org/city/en/depts/dca/
supp_info/chicago_s_publicart-
crownfountaininmillenniumpark

**DAVENPORT'S PIANO BAR
AND CABARET**
1383 N Milwaukee Ave,
Chicago, IL 60622
davenportspianobar.com

DEARBORN STATION
47 W Polk St,
Chicago, IL 60605
dearbornstation.com

DUNLAYS ON THE SQUARE
3137 W Logan Blvd,
Chicago, IL 60647
dunlaysonthesquare.com

ELEVEN CITY DINER
1112 S Wabash Ave,
Chicago, IL 60605
elevencitydiner.com

**FIELD MUSEUM OF NATURAL
HISTORY**
1400 S Lake Shore Dr,
Chicago, IL 60605
fieldmuseum.org

FIREPLACE INN
1448 N Wells St,
Chicago, IL 60610
fireplaceinn.com

FLAMINGO (SCULPTURE)
50 W Adams St,
Chicago, IL 60610

**FOUNTAIN OF TIME
(SCULPTURE)**
6000 S Cottage Grove Ave,
Chicago, IL 60637

FOUR SEASONS (MOSAIC)
10 S Dearborn St,
Chicago, IL 60603

FUDGE POT
1532 N Wells St,
Chicago, IL 60610
thefudgepotchicago.com

GERMANIA CLUB BUILDING
108 W Germania Pl,
Chicago, IL 60610
cityofchicago.org/content/dam/city/
depts/zlup/Historic_Preservation/
Publications/Germania_Club_Bldg.
pdf

GLUNZ TAVERN
1202 N Wells St,
Chicago, IL 60610
glunztavern.com

**HALLOWEEN HALLWAY
COSTUME SHOP**
1355 N Milwaukee Ave,
Chicago, IL 60622
halloweenhallway.com

HAROLD WASHINGTON LIBRARY
400 S State St,
Chicago, IL 60605
chipublib.org/locations/15

HARRY CARAY'S TAVERN
Chicago Children's Museum,
700 E Grand Ave,
Chicago, IL 60611
harrycarays.com

HENRY B. CLARKE HOUSE
1827 S Indiana Ave,
Chicago, IL 60616
cityofchicago.org/city/en/depts/dca/
supp_info/clarke_house_museum

HOT CHOCOLATE
1747 N Damen Ave,
Chicago, IL 60647
hotchocolatechicago.com

HOUSE OF BLUES
329 N Dearborn St,
Chicago, IL 60654
houseofblues.com/Chicago

HUMBOLDT PARK
1400 N Sacramento Ave,
Chicago, IL 60622
chicagoparkdistrict.com/parks/
humboldtpark

IGUANA CAFE
517–519 N Halsted St,
Chicago, IL 60622
iguanacafe.com

**ILLINOIS CENTENNIAL
MONUMENT**
3150 W Logan Blvd,
Chicago, IL 60647
logansquarepreservation.org

JUDY MAXWELL HOME
1349 N Wells St,
Chicago, IL 60610
judymaxwellhome.com

KOKOROKOKO
1323 N Milwaukee Ave,
Chicago, IL 60622
kokorokokovintage.com

LA PETITE FOLIE
1504 E 55th St,
Chicago, IL 60615
lapetitefolie.com

LE PAIN QUOTIDIEN
1562 N Wells St,
Chicago, IL 60610
lepainquotidien.com

LINCOLN PARK CONSERVATORY
2391 N Stockton Dr,
Chicago, IL 60614
lincolnparkconservancy.org

LINCOLN PARK ZOO
2001 N Clark St,
Chicago, IL 60614
lpzoo.org

LOGAN SQUARE FARMERS MARKET
2755 N Milwaukee Ave,
Chicago, IL 60647
logansquarefarmersmarket.org

LOU MALNATI'S
805 S State St,
Chicago, IL 60605
loumalnatis.com

LOVELY KITCHEN & CAFE
1130 N Milwaukee Ave,
Chicago, IL 60622
lovelykitchenandcafe.com

LULA CAFE
2537 N Kedzie Ave,
Chicago, IL 60647
lulacafe.com

MANSUETO LIBRARY
University of Chicago,
1100 E 57th St,
Chicago, IL 60637
lib.uchicago.edu/mansueto

MARCO FLESERI
1422 N Milwaukee Ave,
Chicago, IL 60622
fleseri.com

MCC CHICAGO
71 W Van Buren St,
Chicago, IL 60605
bop.gov/locations/institutions/ccc/
index.jsp

MEDICI ON 57TH
1327 E 57th St,
Chicago, IL 60637
medici57.com

MIDWAY PLAISANCE
1130 Midway Plaisance,
Chicago, IL 60637
chicagoparkdistrict.com/parks/
Midway-Plaisance-Park

MILK & HONEY
1920 W Division St,
Chicago, IL 60622
milkandhoneycafe.com

MON AMI GABI
Belden Stratford,
2300 N Lincoln Park W,
Chicago, IL 60614
monamigabi.com

MUSEUM OF CONTEMPORARY ART
220 E Chicago Ave,
Chicago, IL 60611
mcachicago.org

MUSEUM OF SCIENCE AND INDUSTRY
5700 S Lake Shore Dr,
Chicago, IL 60637
msichicago.org

MYOPIC BOOKS
1564 N Milwaukee Ave,
Chicago, IL 60622
myopicbookstore.com

NAVY PIER
600 E Grand Ave,
Chicago, IL 60611
navypier.com

NEW WAVE COFFEE
3103 W Logan Blvd,
Chicago, IL 60647
newwavecoffee.com

NOOKIES
1746 N Wells St,
Chicago, IL 60614
nookieschicago.com

NORTH AVENUE BEACH BOATHOUSE
1603 N Lake Shore Dr,
Chicago, IL 60611
castawayschicago.com

OAK + FORT
1715 N Damen Ave,
Chicago, IL 60647
oakandfort.com

OAK STREET BEACH
1000 N Lake Shore Dr,
Chicago, IL 60611
cpdbeaches.com/beaches/oak-
street-beach

OLD TOWN ALE HOUSE
219 W North Ave,
Chicago, IL 60610
theoldtownalehouse.com

OLD TOWN POUR HOUSE
1419 N Wells St,
Chicago, IL 60610
oldtownpourhouse.com

ORIGINAL MOTHER'S
26 W Division St,
Chicago, IL 60610
originalmothers.com

ORIGINAL PANCAKE HOUSE
2020 N Lincoln Park West,
Chicago, IL 60614
originalpancakehouse.com

OVERFLOW COFFEE BAR
1550 S State St,
Chicago, IL 60605
overflowcoffeebar.org

PALMER HOUSE
17 E Monroe St,
Chicago, IL 60603
palmerhousehiltonhotel.com

PIECE BREWERY & PIZZERIA
1927 W North Ave,
Chicago, IL 60622
piecechicago.com

POLISH MUSEUM OF AMERICA
984 N Milwaukee Ave,
Chicago, IL 60642
polishmuseumofamerica.org

POLK BROS FOUNTAIN
600 E Grand Ave,
Chicago, IL 60611
navypier.com/polk-bros-park

POLONIA TRIANGLE
Milwaukee and Ashland Aves,
chicagopolishtriangle.com

PUERTO RICAN ARTS ALLIANCE
3000 N Elbridge Ave,
Chicago, IL 60618
praachicago.org

QUIMBY'S
1854 W North Ave,
Chicago, IL 60622
quimbys.com

RENO CHICAGO
2607 N Milwaukee Ave,
Chicago, IL 60647
renochicago.com

REVOLUTION BREWING
2323 N Milwaukee Ave,
Chicago, IL 60647
revbrew.com

RICHARD J. DALEY CENTER
50 W Washington St,
Chicago, IL 60602
thedaleycenter.com

R.J. GRUNTS
2056 N Lincoln Park West,
Chicago, IL 60614
rjgruntschicago.com

ROBIE HOUSE
5757 S Woodlawn Ave,
Chicago, IL 60637
cal.flwright.org/tours/robie

ROCKEFELLER CHAPEL
5850 S Woodlawn Ave,
Chicago, IL 60637
rockefeller.uchicago.edu

ROUTE 66
Lake Shore Dr and Jackson Dr,
Chicago, IL

SECOND CITY
Pipers Alley Mall,
1616 N Wells St,
Chicago, IL 60614
secondcity.com

SHEDD AQUARIUM
1200 S Lake Shore Dr,
Chicago, IL 60605
sheddaquarium.org

SHIT FOUNTAIN (SCULPTURE)
1001 N Wolcott Ave,
Chicago, IL 60622

SOFI RESTAURANT
616 S Dearborn St,
Chicago, IL 60605
sofichicago.com

SPICE HOUSE
1512 N Wells St,
Chicago, IL 60610
thespicehouse.com

SPOKE & BIRD
205 E 18th St,
Chicago, IL 60616
spokeandbird.com

STANDING LINCOLN (STATUE)
Lincoln Park,
Chicago, IL 60614

STATE STREET GALLERY
Robert Morris University,
401 South State St,
Chicago, IL 60605
robertmorris.edu/artgallery

STEVE MADDEN
1553 N Milwaukee Ave,
Chicago, IL 60622
stevemadden.com

THE J. PARKER
1816 N Clark St,
Chicago, IL 60614
jparkerchicago.com

THE PROMONTORY
5311 S Lake Park Ave W,
Chicago, IL 60615
promontorychicago.com

TONI PATISSERIE & CAFE
65 E Washington St,
Chicago, IL 60602
tonipatisserie.com

TOPO GIGIO
1516 N Wells St,
Chicago, IL 60610
topogigiochicago.com

TRANSPORTATION BUILDING
600 S Dearborn St,
Chicago, IL 60605
transportationbuilding.org

TUTTO ITALIANO
501 S Wells St,
Chicago, IL 60607
tuttostogo.com

VALOIS
1518 E 53rd St,
Chicago, IL 60615
valoisrestaurant.com

VALUE PAWN
1219 N Ashland Ave,
Chicago, IL 60622
valuepawnchicago.com

VOLUMES BOOKCAFE
1474 N Milwaukee Ave,
Chicago, IL 60622
volumesbooks.com

WALNUT ROOM
Macy's, 111 N State St,
Chicago, IL 60602
macysrestaurants.com/walnut-room

WATER TOWER
806 N Michigan Ave,
Chicago, IL 60611
cityofchicago.org/city/en/depts/dca/
supp_info/city_gallery_in_thehis-
toricwatertower

WATER TOWER PLACE
835 N Michigan Ave,
Chicago, IL 60611
shopwatertower.com

WEBSTER'S WINE BAR
2601 N Milwaukee Ave,
Chicago, IL 60647
websterwinebar.com

WICKER PARK
1425 N Damen Ave,
Chicago, IL 60622
chicagoparkdistrict.com/parks/
Wicker-Park

WILDBERRY PANCAKES & CAFE
130 E Randolph St,
Chicago, IL 60601
wildberrycafe.com

WOMAN MADE GALLERY
685 N Milwaukee Ave,
Chicago, IL 60642
womanmade.org

WOODED ISLAND
Jackson Park, 1793 E Hayes Dr,
Chicago, IL 60649
chicagoparkdistrict.com/parks/
jackson-park

YOLK
1120 S Michigan Ave,
Chicago, IL 60605
eatyolk.com

ZANIES COMEDY CLUB
1548 N Wells St,
Chicago, IL 60610
zanies.com/Chicago

BIKE SHOPS, CLUBS, RACES AND VENUES

ACTIVE TRANSPORTATION ALLIANCE
9 W Hubbard St, #402,
Chicago, IL 60654
activetrans.org

BIG MARSH PARK
11559 S Stony Island Ave,
Chicago, IL 60633
bigmarsh.org

BIKE AND ROLL
239 E Randolph St,
Chicago, IL 60601
bikeandroll.com/chicago

BIKE FIX-IT STATION
415 N Milwaukee Ave,
Chicago, IL 60654
paramountroom.com/about-us

BOBBY'S BIKE HIKE
540 N Lake Shore Dr,
Chicago, IL 60611
bobbysbikehike.com

BOULEVARD BIKES
2535 N Kedzie Blvd,
Chicago, IL 60647
boulevardbikeshop.com

CHICAGO BIKE RACING
chicagobikeracing.com

CHICAGO CYCLING CLUB
chicagocyclingclub.org

CRITICAL MASS
chicagocriticalmass.org

DES PLAINES RIVER TRAIL
15601 W Russell Rd,
Wadsworth, IL 60083
lcfpd.org/dprt

DIVVY
divvybikes.com

DJ'S BIKE DOCTOR
1344 E 55th St,
Chicago, IL 60615
djsbikedoctor.com

ED RUDOLPH VELODROME
1479 Maple Ave,
Northbrook, IL 60062
northbrookcyclecommittee.org

ILLINOIS CYCLING ASSOCIATION
illinoiscycling.org

ILLINOIS PRAIRIE PATH
ipp.org

INTELLIGENTSIA CUP
intelligentsiacup.com

J.C. LIND BIKE CO.
1311 N Wells St,
Chicago, IL 60610
jclindbikes.com

MAYOR'S BICYCLE ADVISORY COUNCIL
121 N LaSalle St,
Chicago, IL 60602
facebook.com/
events/1680214425636942

MORAINE HILLS STATE PARK
1510 S River Rd,
McHenry, IL 60051
dnr.illinois.gov/Parks/Pages/
MoraineHills

OLD PLANK ROAD TRAIL
oprt.org/maps.htm

PALOS FOREST PRESERVE TRAIL
fpdcc.com

RAPHA CHICAGO
1514 N Milwaukee Ave,
Chicago, IL 60622
pages.rapha.cc/clubs/rapha-
chicago

SLOW ROLL CHICAGO
899 S Plymouth Ct, #110,
Chicago, IL 60605
slowrollchicago.org

THE GARDEN
3400 N Rockwell St,
Chicago, IL 60618
thegardenjumps.com

UNIVERSITY OF CHICAGO VELO CLUB
ucvc.uchicago.edu

VILLAGE CYCLE CENTER
1337 N Wells St,
Chicago, IL 60610
villagecycle.com

WASHINGTON PARK VELODROME
Washington Rd and 22nd Ave,
Kenosha, WI 53140
northbrookcyclecommittee.org

WATERFALL GLEN FOREST TRAIL
Lemont, IL 60439
dupageforest.com/Conservation/
Forest_Preserves/Waterfall_Glen

XXX RACING-ATHLETICO
xxxracing.org

OTHER USEFUL SITES

AMTRAK
amtrak.com

MIDWAY INTERNATIONAL AIRPORT
5700 S Cicero Ave,
Chicago, IL 60638
flychicago.com/midway

O'HARE INTERNATIONAL AIRPORT
10000 W O'Hare Ave,
Chicago, IL 60666
flychicago.com/ohare

UNION STATION
225 S Canal St,
Chicago, IL 60606
chicagounionstation.com

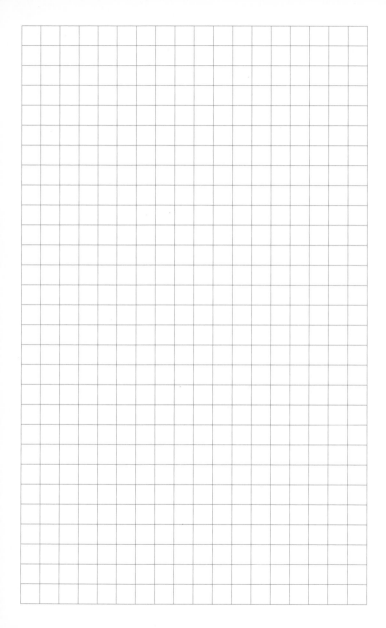

NOTES

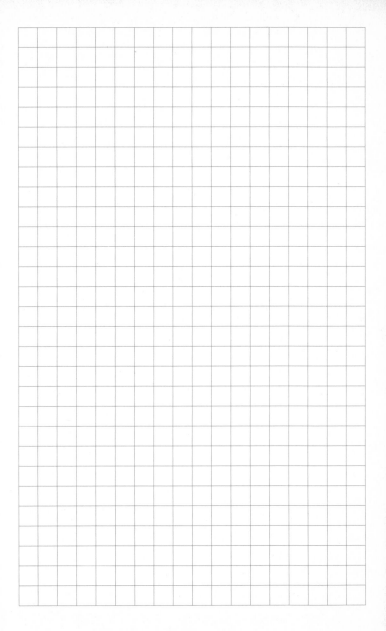

NOTES

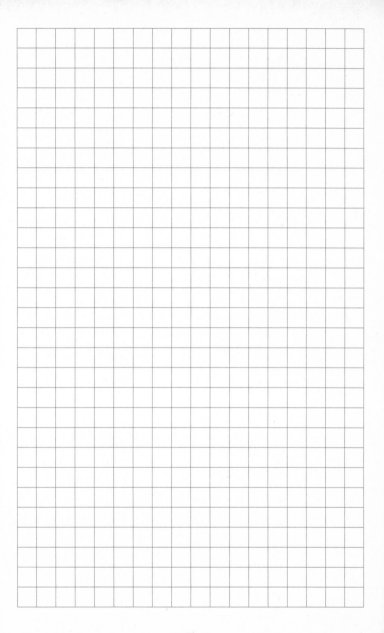

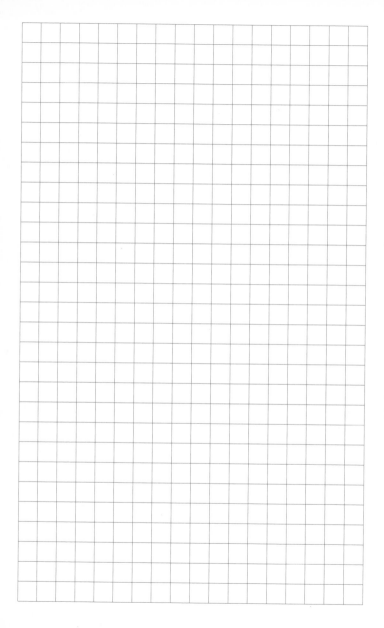

NOTES

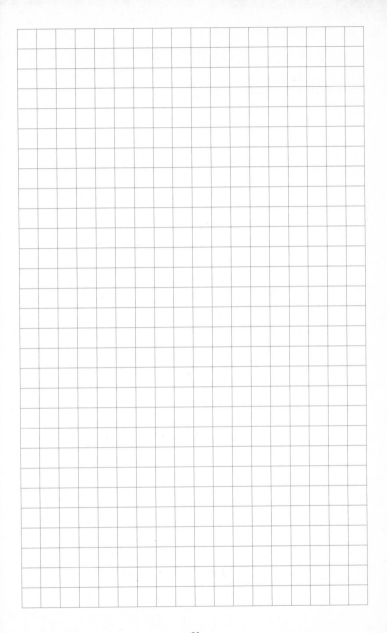

NOTES

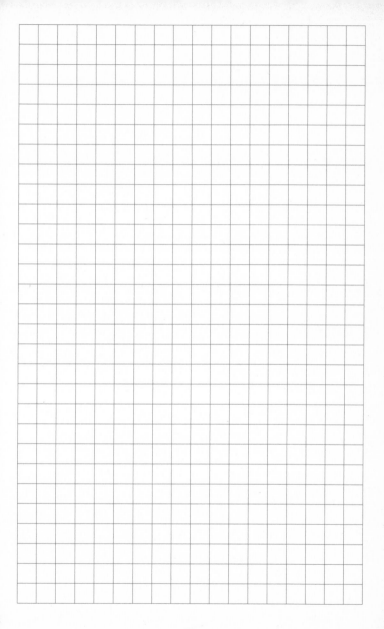

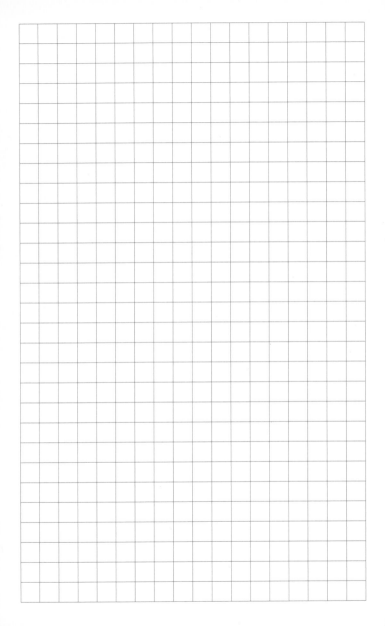

NOTES

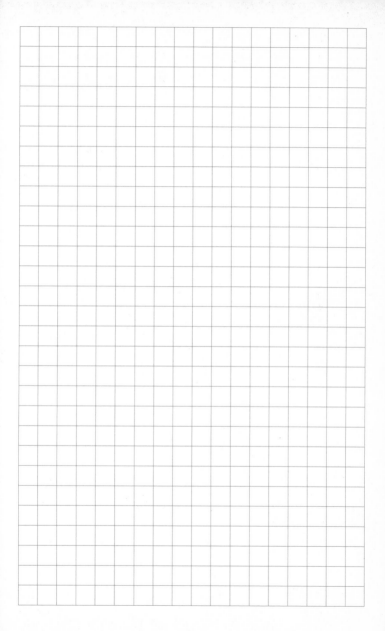